Time

Contents

Written by Brian Roberts

Introduction

We order our lives by time. We are nearly always aware of the time, from the moment we get out of bed until we go to sleep at night. Time lets us know when to do things and for how long.

Sun

It takes one year for the Earth to travel around the sun.

Measuring Time

Time is measured by the Earth's movements.

It takes one year for the planet Earth to make one complete trip around the sun.

As the Earth goes around the sun, it also spins like a top. A day and night pass each time the Earth makes one complete spin. This is called a solar day.

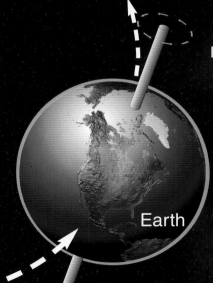

It takes one 24-hour day for the Earth to make one complete spin on its axis.

Earth

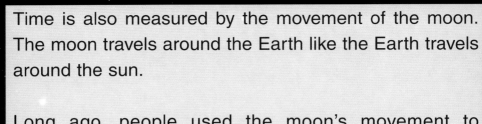

Time is also measured by the movement of the moon. The moon travels around the Earth like the Earth travels around the sun.

Long ago, people used the moon's movement to measure time. The time it took the moon to make one complete trip around the Earth was called one moon.

Today, one moon is called a month. We still use the month as a unit of time, but it is not exactly the time it takes the moon to make one trip around the Earth.

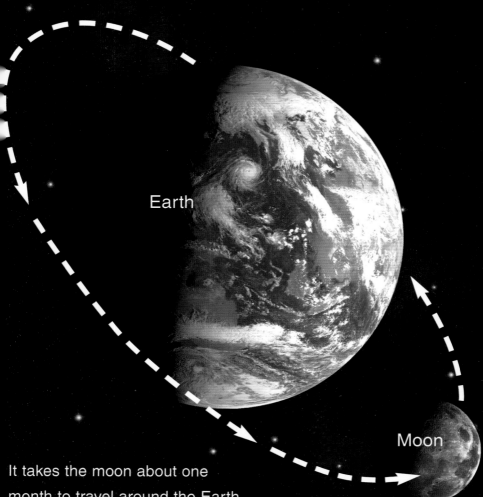

Earth

Moon

It takes the moon about one month to travel around the Earth.

People have been looking for ways to keep track of time for thousands of years.

First, people tracked larger units of time, such as the passing of seasons and days and nights, but they always looked for ways to divide time into smaller units.

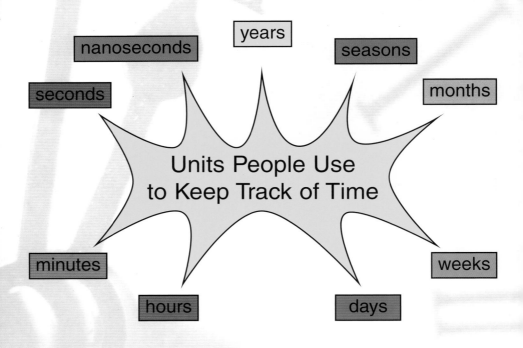

seconds
nanoseconds
years
seasons
months

Units People Use to Keep Track of Time

minutes
hours
days
weeks

They started with calendars to measure years and seasons. Then years were divided into months, and months into weeks, and weeks into days.

Eventually, days were divided into hours, minutes, seconds, and even nanoseconds.

Calculations of One Year	
Unit	Number each year
months	12
weeks	52
days	365*
hours	8,760*
minutes	525,600*
seconds	31,536,000*
nanoseconds	31,536,000,000,000,000*

* add one day for a leap year

The Calendar

There are many different calendars used in the world, but most follow the movements of the sun and moon.

The Egyptians were the first people to use a calendar. Much like today's calendar year, the Egyptian calendar year was 365 days long.

The Aztec calendar year was also 365 days. It had 18 months of 20 days each. Wood or stone carvings showed symbols of the days.

Aztec Calendar

People were always trying to improve the accuracy of the calendar.

The calendar we use today is based on the Roman calendar. Julius Caesar introduced the Julian calendar with a 365-day year. But because a year is about six hours longer than 365 days, the Julian calendar was slightly inaccurate. An extra day had to be added every four years.

A year with 366 days is called a leap year.

Modern Leap Years

1992
1996
2000
2004
2008
2012
2016
2020

About 400 years ago, Pope Gregory XIII revised the Julian calendar to make it even more accurate.

Today, the Gregorian calendar is used in most countries.

March from the Gregorian Calendar

March

M	T	W	T	F	S	S
			1	2	3	4
5	6	7	8	9	10	11
12	13	14	15	16	17	18
19	20	21	22	23	24	25
26	27	28	29	30	31	

Although the Gregorian calendar is the official calendar of China, the Chinese also use the Chinese calendar to mark festivals.

The Chinese calendar has a 12-year cycle, with 12 signs to represent each year of the cycle. Each sign is represented by a different animal. The signs repeat every 12 years.

The Chinese Calendar

Shadow Clocks

There is some evidence that shadow clocks, or sundials, are some of the oldest devices used to measure time.

The most common shadow clock is the horizontal sundial. It is found in gardens all around the world.

Shadow clocks are found all around the world.

The sundial has two parts – a flat disk, or dial plane, and an extension from the top of the disk, which is called a gnomon. The gnomon casts a shadow on the dial plane. As the sun's position changes, the shadow falls on different numbers along the edge of the disk. By reading the number where the shadow falls, people can tell what the time is.

People can tell the time by reading where the shadow falls.

Make a Shadow Clock

Materials

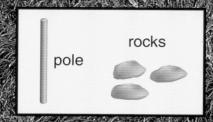

pole

rocks

- Pole
- Rocks

Directions

1 Find a sunny place and put the pole into the ground.

2 Begin in the early morning. At the beginning of the hour, place a rock on the ground where the end of the shadow falls.

8 o'clock

7 o'clock

3 Then, every hour, place another rock on the ground where the end of the shadow falls.

4 At the end of the day, notice how the length of the shadow has changed with each hour.

9 o'clock

Sand Clocks

Over 600 years ago, sand clocks measured time by how long it took sand, or salt, to pass from the top container to the bottom container.

The container's size and the width of the opening determined the amount of time it took the sand to pass from the top container to the bottom.

When all the sand had passed through, sand clocks could be turned over to start again.

Sand clocks measure time.

Sand clocks used to measure one hour were called hourglasses. There were other sizes of sand clock used to measure other periods of time.

Sand clocks that measure an hour are called hourglasses.

Make a Sand Clock

You can make a sand clock by following the easy steps shown below.

Materials

- 2 clear plastic soda or water bottles of the same size
- Masking or duct tape
- Medium-sized nail
- Fine mesh screen
- Hammer
- Clean, dry sand or salt

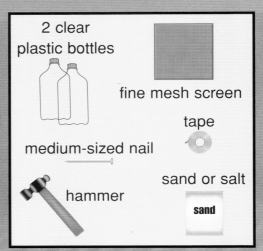

2 clear plastic bottles

fine mesh screen

medium-sized nail

tape

hammer

sand or salt

sand

Directions

1 Sift the sand through the mesh screen.

2 Half fill one of the bottles with sand.

3 Tape the two caps together.

4 Use the nail and hammer to make a small, smooth hole through the middle of both caps.

5 Screw the cap on the bottle with the sand in it. Next, screw the other bottle onto the other cap.

6 Decide how much time you want to measure. Note the time as you turn the sand clock over.

7 When the amount of time passes that you want to measure, turn the sand clock on its side. Unscrew the bottle that was on top. Remove any sand that did not pass through the opening. Screw the bottle back on.

Now you have a sand clock that measures a set amount of time. If you want it to measure more or less time, add or remove sand.

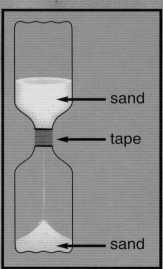

sand

tape

sand

Candle Clocks

Hundreds of years ago, people in China learned that time could be measured by how long it takes a candle to burn. They used thick candles to measure longer periods of time and thin candles to measure shorter periods of time.

Candles would either have lines marked on their sides, or they would be made of alternate wax stripes.

Thick candles for longer periods

Thin candles for shorter periods

lines

alternate wax stripes

For instance, the lines or stripes of wax might be marked with 30-minute intervals. Each time the candle burned for 30 minutes, it would reach a new mark or a new layer of wax.

Accuracy depended on having candles of the same thickness from top to bottom.

same thickness from top to bottom

Make a Candle Clock

You can make a candle clock of your own by getting the materials listed and following the steps below.

Materials

- Tall candle about 1 inch (2.5cm) in diameter (make sure it is the same thickness from top to bottom)
- Shallow pan
- Felt-tip marker
- Ruler
- Clay

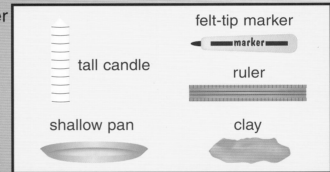

tall candle

felt-tip marker

marker

ruler

shallow pan

clay

Directions

1 Use the ruler to measure the candle.

2 Use the clay to hold the candle upright in the pan.

3 Burn the candle for 30 minutes, and then blow it out.

4 Measure the length and subtract the length from the first measurement. This gives you the length the candle will burn in 30 minutes.

5 Mark lines on the candle for several 30-minute time intervals. You can write numbers on each line from top to bottom to keep track of the number of time periods that pass.

Your candle clock can be marked for any time interval by following steps 3, 4, and 5, and burning the candle for a shorter or longer time.

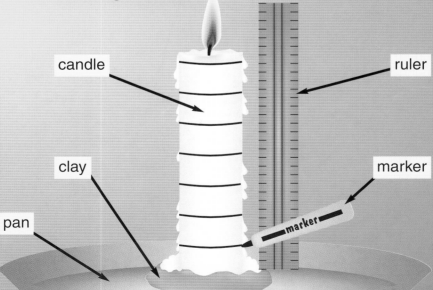

candle

ruler

clay

marker

pan

marker

Water Clocks

The flow of water was used thousands of years ago to tell time. People in China, Egypt, and other areas invented many water clocks.

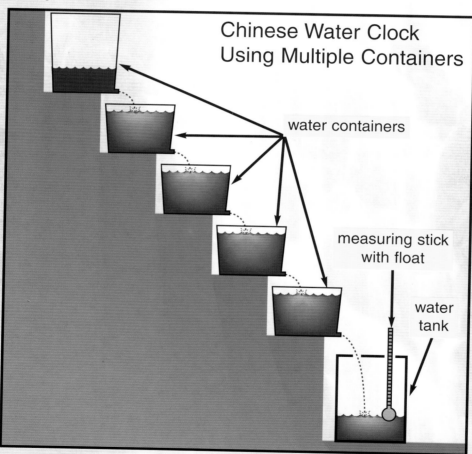

Chinese Water Clock Using Multiple Containers

water containers

measuring stick with float

water tank

The Chinese invented a water clock that was made of a series of containers. The containers were placed with each one higher than the other, so that a higher container would empty into the one below it.

The water emptied into a tank at the end of the row of containers. A float with an upright stick would rise in the tank as more water entered from the bottom container. Numbers on the stick told how much time had passed.

The flow into the tank was even because the bottom container in the series was filled by water flowing from the containers above. The even flow caused the float to rise steadily.

Make a Chinese Water Clock

You can make a model of a Chinese water clock by following the steps below.

Materials

- 5 large clear plastic soda or water bottles
- Medium-sized nail
- Hammer
- Ruler
- Felt-tip marker
- Water

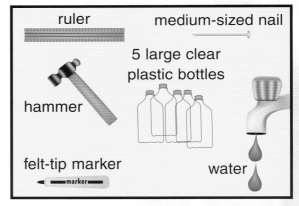

Directions

1 Have an adult cut the bottom 2 inches (5 cm) from four of the bottles and the top off the fifth bottle.

2 Use the hammer and nail to punch a small hole in the middle of four of the caps. Screw the caps on the four bottles with tops.

3 Put the bottle without a top on a flat surface. Half fill one of the other bottles with water and place it top down into the bottom bottle.

4 Continue half filling each of the remaining bottles with water and stack them one on top of the other as shown in the picture.

5 Use a watch or clock to time the water dripping into the bottom bottle.

6 After two minutes, make a mark at the top of the water level. Continue timing and marking every two minutes.

7 Use the ruler to check if the marks are the same distance apart. Then make additional marks on the bottom bottle to complete your time scale.

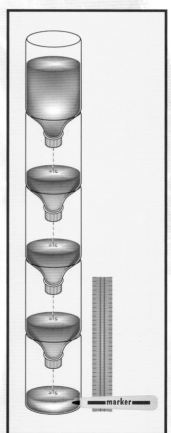

Mechanical Clocks

The first mechanical clocks worked by using a falling weight. The weight hung from a rope wrapped around a small metal drum. As the weight slowly unwound, the drum turned.

The drum turned two gears that moved the hour hand. When the weight reached the bottom, it had to be wound around the drum again. Eventually, another gear was added to turn a second hand.

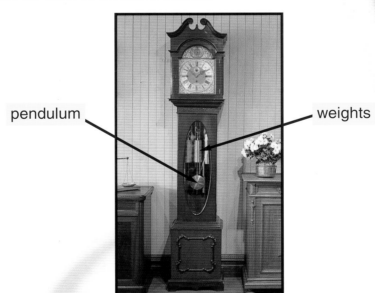

pendulum   weights

Some older clocks had a long swinging piece called a pendulum hanging beneath the face of the clock. This pendulum kept the weight falling at a steady rate, so that the clock kept time accurately.

Weights were replaced with springs that would slowly unwind and turn gears. Springs meant that clocks could be made smaller, and eventually pocket watches and wristwatches were made.

The parts inside a wristwatch

Electricity allowed wind-up clocks to be replaced with electrical clocks. They could be plugged into electrical outlets or powered with batteries. Today, most watches are powered by small batteries.

High-Tech Time

Special clocks and watches can measure time in very small, accurate units.

Scientists need accurate timing for their experiments.

Many sports are timed in fractions of a second. Stopwatches are used to get accurate timing. In some races, one-tenth of a second can mean the difference between winning and losing.

stopwatch

The most accurate clock is the atomic clock. It is so accurate that it loses only one second in over a million years.

Unveiling of the atomic clock

Index